UNFETTERED SOUL

Poems and Contemplations on Recovery

DARLENE LANCER

Printed in the United States of America
First Printing 2024
ISBN No. 979-8-218-56341-7
Carousel Books
Santa Monica, California
www.whatiscodependency.com

Table of Contents

Introduction

Cry, laugh, exclaim hurray and aha!

Unfettered Soul: Poems and Contemplations on Recovery is a heartfelt collection of personal poems written by me and nine other contributors that explore our grief, triumphs, and revelations along our journey to self-love, healing, and transformation. This profound inquiry into soul reclamation delves into the multifaceted nature of the psyche, offering sensitive wisdom into personal growth and self-discovery.

For me, crafting a poem is a journey that uncovers, clarifies, and releases complex feelings and experiences. As a child, I began reading and writing poetry, which has since become a gratifying and powerful tool for healing and self-discovery.

This introspective process often starts with a reflection on a feeling, a thought, or an observation in nature, sometimes unfolding as a metaphor that mirrors inchoate ideas or emotions. The struggle to find the right words and rhythm holds significance. As I immerse in the process, it intensifies, distractions fade, and new insights emerge. Each draft deepens my exploration and becomes both cathartic and transformative. The culmination brings clarity, a sense of accomplishment, and greater understanding of myself and the human condition.

Healing is not linear or categorizable but is an obscure odyssey that meanders, stagnates, and has its ups and downs. It warps time, intertwining our past and present, along with our perspectives, relationships, and emotional struggles.

Despite this complexity, I organized the poems into six sections: *Perspectives, Relationships, Angst, Change and Transformation, Faith,* and *Self-Love and Healing.* Section headings are somewhat arbitrary. There are poems about relationships that also touch on healing or angst and poems about depression that is often preparatory to transition to something new. Each section concludes with insightful essays for self-reflection. They follow the poems to allow you to read them without any bias or preconceived interpretation.

Perspectives—how we define ourselves and our worldview—is often arbitrary and shaped by our early experiences and the narratives we construct around our identity and the environment. Whether we see our life as half-full or half-empty, the world and people as safe or dangerous, or time as our friend or our enemy substantially impacts us. Frequently, our perspectives determine our behavior, magnify our anxieties, and cause our negative thoughts and inner conflict.

Relationships play a crucial role in our growth, as they reveal our wounded places, starting with our parents who influence how we love. Early parental interactions influence our attachment style in adult relationships. Unmet childhood needs and intimacy patterns can lead us to self-sacrifice, confuse love with longing, and hamper healthy inter-dependency. Some people lose themselves in relationships or choose to be alone to retain their autonomy. Others resolve this dilemma by having short, serial relationships, pursuing someone unavailable, or using an addiction to create distance. We may need to redefine love, our needs and expectations, and how we interact with loved ones. Many of the poems in this section explore painful lessons and relationships as growth opportunities.

Angst may visit us in the form of anxiety, isolation, depression, and despair. Past trauma that lingers in the shadows exacerbates our pain and complicates our journey. Our greatest suffering usually arises from distorted thinking, shame, or loss of our dreams, abilities, or loved ones. When we feel rejected or lose a relationship, the poignant shame of feeling unloved, unlovable, or unwanted is magnified. Yet, these painful experiences illuminate wounds we need to heal.

Our soul cries out for *Change* when our lives are out of alignment, but change isn't easy. When I began my journey over 40 years ago, I read a book entitled *Courage to Change.* At that time, I never thought about courage, nor associated it with change. But indeed it has taken courage and the support of mentors who went before me. We need courage to let go of familiar yet unhelpful patterns and defenses that have kept us safe. We usually resist until the ongoing unhappiness with ourselves, our relationship, or our work prompts us to change. Fear can blind us to our potential for growth, but recognizing that our distress beckons transformation motivates us to take action. Courage to change our attitudes and behaviors is essential for personal growth, as is accepting responsibility for our happiness.

Faith emerges as a guiding light on this journey, supporting transitions, and inviting us to trust in the unknown. Praying for a specific outcome may stem from a desire for control, often driven by fear. Yet, cultivating true faith embraces uncertainty with patience and opens our heart to the ever-changing aliveness of the present. It helps us acknowledge instances where we're powerless and to relinquish the need to manage every aspect of our lives. In doing so, we become empowered to take meaningful action.

Eventually, our journey leads us to the heart of *Self-love*, teaching us that healing begins with compassion for ourselves. Seeking external solutions to alleviate our suffering only provides temporary relief. True healing requires self-reflection and self-acceptance. We often underestimate the impact of a loving response to ourselves. It involves deep listening, honoring our feelings, setting boundaries, and nurturing our emotional and physical well-being.

Self-compassion allows us to move beyond self-criticism and discover our true self, fostering resilience and inner peace. By opening our heart and mind to the present moment, we channel the intrinsic energy that unites us with the fabric of life. We become happier, calmer, and more accepting of people and the vicissitudes of life.

Recovery is not a destination but a continual process of transformation—an ongoing adventure, rich with opportunities for growth and self-discovery. Through this journey, I've gained inspiration, transforming insecurity into strength and emotional resilience. Whether you're navigating the challenges of recovery, seeking a deeper understanding of yourself, or on a quest for solace, inspiration, or transformation, *Unfettered Soul* offers a guiding, uplifting light through darkness. I hope that by sharing this journey, you find insight and encouragement to reflect on your experiences, reclaim your inner strength, and embrace the beauty of your unfettered soul.

I'm grateful to the men and women who have graciously contributed their soulful poetry, expressing their pain, faith, and recovery: Suzanne Henderson, Owen Reynolds, Ole Kevin Rodberg, David Morris, Arianna Winkle, P.S Lutz, Mike Gormley, Ann Fuller, and my brother, Dr. Jason W. Brown.

PERSPECTIVES

Who

Unlike Descartes, I'm not so sure
If, or who "I" am,
Or who's the "I" who questions this,
Or when this "I" began.

Is the "I" who talks to me,
Different from "I" who listens?
"I" can't be found in the brain,
And it wanders off in sleep,
But soon returns to weave my dreams,
Then revives memories of it "I" keep.

But is the "I" who remembers
the antecedent "I" gone-by?
Should my memory dull and fail,
Would "I" too wane null and die?

Does this "I" persist in coma,
Or alter in a trance
Yet evaporate when lovers' kiss
or meditate on emptiness?

Perhaps this "I" comes and goes,
With thoughts arising from the mist,

UNFETTERED SOUL

Like stars that fill the evening sky
That fade at dawn, though still exist.
So is this "I" my own construction,
Made of thoughts and memory?
Or if it's more, then who creates
Cosmic dust in our anatomy?

By Darlene Lancer

Sunset by the Sea

No words can woo a restful peace
As does sunset by the sea.
The sun shines a brilliant highway
That spans from shore to sky.

Shadows invade the glittery beam,
Until consumed by waves
That slowly snuff its golden gleam
And devour the sun into milky blue.

The vivid path glowed so bright and real.
Never truly does it dissolve,
If surely it was there,
Even by reflection only.
But its source vanished
In the waters whence it came.

Each dawn the sea births the sun
That bears life to the sea and path –
Till mother and child dissolve as one.

An illusory lane traced by blinding light.
So seductive, so beautiful and bold,
Seemingly secure enough to walk on.

UNFETTERED SOUL

What if all of time compressed
Within that sunset hour
When the path emerged then faded in the brine?
Then we might never see the sun leave the sky,
Nor die, enveloped by the sea.

And perhaps if we lived longer and more slowly,
Or were tall enough to glimpse
Beyond the corners of the sea
To watch the sun live on
And not daily disappear,
Then some paths that burn so brightly
And goals that glow distinctly,
Would vanish when seen in total view,
And we would laugh and rest as we may do,
When we sip the peace of sunset by the sea.

By Darlene Lancer

Perfection

Like a fool insane, I caught a glimpse, and starving I pursue,
So close I get, the gap declines, it's just within my grip.
It's so perfect, porting symmetry, clean and pure and new.
Inevitably though, by now I know,
Through my fingers it will slip.

I never stop, by fate or fault, it's destined to be my role.
This endless cycle, a tiring loop, of chase, entrap and fail,
With perfect timing, the notion floats, it's absence of a soul,
Like a fool once more, I try again, maybe now I will prevail.

Endurance wanes, as so oft times past, in reality and in dream,
Of this construct, this perception false,
So desperately that I hold.
How perfect the idea at first, a resolution it may seem,
Standing by its own weight, or lack thereof, it will surely fold.

What a wonderful place, if so allowed, a being can become.
Internal strength and strength of wisdom, allowing to perceive,
New alignments of those traps
That with ease would strip my freedom.
And so, I fear, a fool once more, it's myself I do deceive.

By Owen Reynolds

Man's Gift

Billions of moons rise and set,
Without effort the stars glide by.
Flowers born to bloom and die,
Without a thought their petals fall.

The passing sun gives us life,
Yet everyday summons death.
With each reply two souls gain breath
And map a path that is their own.

Rainbows bless each leaving storm.
Centillion waves crash on the shore,
And hungry birds fly south once more,
As one by one the seasons pass.

In autumn, rustling leaves turn brown.
Wind sways the trees and grasses blow.
Owls' hoots meet the winter night,
And bird songs greet spring's melting snow.

Why must man weigh his acts wrong or right,
Smother drives, and know defeat,
Bear jealousy, loss, hate, and shame,
Be judged, enslaved, coveted, and outcast,

PERSPECTIVES

Forever repent the past unforgiven,
Kill one another and ravish beauty?

For the gift of imagination.

By Darlene Lancer

War and Peace

To catch a twilight surf,
I collapse and rest beneath the palms.
Wet salt air subdues my city breath.

The vast horizon calms my treadmill mind.
A sinking blaze of purple, pink, and orange skies
Revives computer weary eyes.

My frozen chest melts and sighs,
While ceaseless tides trek through time.
Whitecaps rise, then disappear to die.
My restive heart ebbs and flows in rhyme.

Seagulls climb and dive to party on the sands.
Beyond the aims of men my view expands.
Then from afar, *Un bel di* serenades
Beloved Earth as it flies through space
While bombs descend on foreign lands.

By Darlene Lancer

A Happiness

By all accounts
I should not be
As happy as I've ever been.

But mine is not
A happiness
That comes in being comforted.

To see me smile,
To hear me laugh:
Not something for the faint of heart

I feel for life.
I don't feel that this life owes me
More than that which comes from living.

By P.S. Lutz

Contemplation

Most of us move through life without reflecting on our perspective, yet it shapes everything—our attitude, actions, and ultimately, our destiny. It influences how we prioritize our values and purpose, view people as safe or dangerous, and see our lives as half full or half empty.

These poems explore just a few of many possible perspectives. Even how we define ourselves is arbitrary. We often tie our identity to our roles, occupations, gender, and sexual preferences. Beyond that, our notion of an enduring, stable "I" is not easily defined, nor tangible. But what would change if we realized our self-conception is a mere construct, as suggested in "Who?"

When we view ourselves subjectively, our problems are magnified because we consider everything in terms of how it affects us personally. However, what if we viewed ourselves through an objective lens as part of a greater, timeless whole? Our problems seem less significant in the grand scheme of things. Life on earth will continue without us and after we die.

A balanced view is prudent. Too much engagement can overwhelm us with worry, while too much detachment can make us feel that nothing matters and our existence is meaningless. Our dilemma is how to live both engaged and detached without denying either viewpoint.

How we view time also impacts our perspective, suggested in "Sunset the Sea." Time seems to expand when we're immersed in the present, slow down when we're waiting or bored, and zips by when we're busy and as we age. If we believe life is a race against time, like the anxious White Rabbit, we may miss out on life and never find true fulfillment.

Our perception of ourselves is often distorted by the inner voices of the critic and perfectionist, as illustrated in "Perfection," which can label us as superior, unlovable, victims, or failures. Many people entirely identify with their inner critic. In recovery, our perspective changes, allowing us to shed false beliefs and habits.

Naturally, we desire positive feelings and experiences. But strong emotions and negative thoughts can overpower us, causing us to think, "I'm a jealous or angry person." How often do we judge things as good or bad, dwell on the past, or worry about the future? Our thoughts and feelings come and go. They're not who we are. This creates inner conflict, reactivity, and dissatisfaction with the present.

Our perspective can shift depending on where we place our attention. I pondered various viewpoints in writing "War and Peace" during the Iraqi war, expanding from the personal to the public, the global, and to an overview from space. Similarly, when we cultivate gratitude, we feel more grateful and consequently are happier—the viewpoint taken in "A Happiness."

If our perspective on life is passive or we have an external locus of control, we tend to feel powerless, believing our lives and happiness are in the hands of fate and other people. With an internal locus of control, we feel empowered to act, knowing that our life and happiness are up to us.

By questioning our beliefs and habitual reactions, we may notice tendencies to worry, seek approval, control, or judge ourselves. As we question our beliefs and habitual reactions, the sources of our worries and judgments are revealed. We can contemplate: Who shaped these beliefs? Might others see things differently? Is there evidence for alternative beliefs? Are my beliefs and actions serving me well? What if I dared to see things differently?

RELATIONSHIPS

Mother Wounds

I'd forgotten that I'd loved her
When she was my world.
I remember only years
Of dismissal and correction.
Unsafe to feel tears packed away.
My silent shield fed her rejection.

Our mother is our first love,
From her mother's mother's belly,
Trauma breathed through generations
Long before our birth.
Her voice echoes in our soma,
Fating love relations and our worth.

She is our first heartbreak
When warmth vanished from her face,
A buried hurt we can't erase.
Seeking to repair that ache
In friends, and pets, and lovers
To be our longed-for mothers.

But we find the flaws she had
Repeated now in others.
They provoke that sad and lonely place
When we hungered for her warm embrace.

RELATIONSHIPS

Ice queen mothers can be cruel,
Play victim, or are never there.
Others harshly rule and meddle everywhere.
Some reign the *fairest of them all*
And treat their daughter like a doll.

Our unique self she cannot see,
But only her reflection.
She squelches our identity
To mold us to perfection.

She faults our likes and how we talk,
Our friends, our clothes, and how we walk.
She's tangled in our brain and cells,
And models how we judge ourselves.

To her we are invisible.
Our sentient needs grow hard to find.
As mother-daughter boundary blurs,
Her rules and ways seep through our mind
To merge our thoughts and wants with hers.

Blind to her fragility,
We fear our mother's anger,
So forsake autonomy and truth
To people-please in place of candor.

Defiance or compliance
Robs our nature bit by bit.
We're trapped within a puzzlement:
Lose our Self or risk abandonment.

UNFETTERED SOUL

Unsure if we or she's to blame,
Judged touchy, spoiled, and selfish,
We live with lies that we're unfit
And guilt we cannot name.

Struggles to individuate
Draw reprimand and penalty
That breed silent, growing hate
And quash our budding liberty.

Her well-meant schemes to dominate
And embed her unlived dreams
Sap our courage and our might
To wake our nascent birthright.

Glass walls us from ourselves and Mother.
We reach though cannot feel each other.
Our primal need remains unfilled
For mother-daughter synchrony.
We try to change and hope she will,
Still clinging to our fantasy.

Perfection cloaks unconfidence.
We dodge the world's and others' eyes.
Our hidden wound intensifies,
Extirpates our innocence,
And shrinks our self-esteem inside.

RELATIONSHIPS

All we want is peace,
To curl up in her arms and rest
Our sobbing heart upon her breast.
Instead, we cry alone, unheard, unseen.

It's our buried Self we must reclaim—
Who we always were.
From her mother's womb we can rebound,
Shed worry that we learned from her,
Resentment that has kept us chained,
And unhealed shame she handed down.

A mother gives us many things
Yet lacks those she's not received:
Tenderness and nurturing,
That we can only grieve.

In our fractured, broken hearts,
Wounded women both are we.
Who must accept each other
To leave behind our legacy.

Give thanks for what she tried to give.
And enjoy the life we have to live.
One day we'll find within our soul
A caring mother who loves us whole.

By Darlene Lancer

Winter

On sunny days, every step
Of thought shrouds the moment,
Vanishing in the slow passage of time,
And I miss the company of men.

On the first breath of winter
The geese leave the pond.
Ice bends the willows.
Life sleeps in the soil.

You know better than I,
Names are like pebbles
Thrown out of the living core
On the dead crust of the earth.

The spirit of the world lies
In the bed of time,
Waiting to be heard
By those who listen.

Help me, friends, to know
The quiet in the wood,
What passes between men,
The pause between words.

By Jason W. Brown, MD
Author of *Love And Other Emotions: On The Process Of Feeling*

Mental Chess

My father taught me checkers,
But Hank taught me chess,
He defined the roles of king and queen,
Of bishop, knight, pawn, and rook
And permitted moves that each one took.

 "Offense is my defense," he'd say.
Everything he did was planned.
He calculated every ploy and play.
Tricked and trapped at every turn,
His strategy I'd never learn.

But then one day I changed the rules
And started doing things my way.
I called his bluff and claimed abuse.
Dumfounded I did not obey,
His gambit up, I flew the roost.

By Darlene Lancer

The Gordian Knot

A bond scarred by guilt and grief
Sewn unspoken in the past
Tied by blood in a common fate,
Three lives marred by shadows cast.

Victims of lies and love and hate,
Trust defiled, years lost apart.
Mother and child split asunder.
Tender limbs torn from the heart.

Now a man I hardly know
Meets me for a while.
I sense there are things that he won't show
Beneath his friendly smile.

I see a wounded teen I left behind
Whom I fear losing once again.
As silent doubt haunts my mind,
I smile, too, with lips half-sealed.

We chat, uplifted for today.
But soon returns my heart concealed
Filled with words I never say.

All parents fret when youth leave home,
Cut the cord to make life their own.
They leave emptiness that's never filled.

But when memories are robbed and few,
Mothers miss the tenderness
Of happy times they knew.

My mind churns crimes I can't acquit
And reruns pain from long ago.
Yet every day I feed it,
I eat the seeds I sow.

To forgive ourselves and one another
For a knotted past we can't undo
Frees this cancer from our family
To recover and begin anew.

By Darlene Lancer

Lost in Eden

She walks barefoot
As the ground kisses her feet.
In her pretty little paradise
She dances along
To her own heartbeat,
Singing life is hard
But love is sweet.

She is the serpent slithering.
She is the apple in the tree.
You could be the devil
And she still loves tenderly.

In the garden of Eden
She is divinity,
Tasting the poison
To uncover the truth.

But why, my darling,
Do you do what you do?
Why, my sweetheart,
Do you keep hurting you?
You don't need to bleed
To know you're alive.

RELATIONSHIPS

Heart explosion,
Self implosion,
Sweet like honey
In the space between
What hurts and what heals
You will find her running.

Quietly now,
She surrenders
Who she has been
To who she is becoming.

By Arianna Winkle

That Old Lady

That old lady? She a killa.
Don't be fooled.
Don't get schooled.
Don't you front.
Don't you play.
She will make you lose your way.

That old lady? She a killa.
Codependent in a villa.
Don't be fooled.
You'll get schooled.
Her "Love" is but a tool.
If you give your will away,
Forever you're her fool.

That old lady rips out souls.
You can't feel it,
But she knows.
Manipulation is her throne,
Scars forever.
You are scorned.

RELATIONSHIPS

That old lady? Many secrets
You can't know,
Won't be shown.
Picture perfect?
It's all fiction.
Narcissism is addiction.

That old lady? She is guiltless.
What's the problem?
What I've done?
What's the difference?
Cause I've lived it.
Outta here, now I've grown.

That old lady? She's a user,
Now a stranger and abuser.

No more games.
No more shame.
Now I'm done.
And left alone.

By David Morris
Contributing Author, *Life After Trauma*

Flying Monkeys

The gathering monkeys,
They stand to attention,
Their queen they must please,
Or face their expulsion.

With their smug upturned faces,
And tongues hanging out,
She sprinkles her graces,
And they're sent on their rout.

There's two of their liking,
Deemed fit to solicit,
Those who are willing,
And worse, those complicit.

And off they will fly,
In pursuit of their game,
By tale and by lie,
To poison a name.

And more often than not,
It passes this way,
A battle lost before fought,
For those caught in the fray.

But my friend, there's a path,
One we must clear,
To withstand this wrath,
And hiding in fear.

It's our love for our fellow,
And power of the mind,
And courage to not follow,
And staying true to our kind.

By Owen Reynolds

The Cost of Love Lost

Spellbound from the start,
For lust or "love" we lose our heart.
A fire lights our chemistry,
Desire and intensity
Confuse love with what's anxiety.

Convincing us that they're *the one,*
Worrying naught for what may come.
Hoping their intent is true,
Ignoring fact and intuition,
We overlook what they lack
And disregard the things we knew
To fabricate our vision.

Romantic hope sweeps us away
While seeking love to keep,
Our morals and our minds may stray.
The price of passion can be steep.

Waning love breeds accusations,
Doubt, deceit, and expectations
For commitments overpromised
And endearments less than honest.

RELATIONSHIPS

Distrust and shock cause bitter breakups,
Wasted grief, and prolonged hurt,
Or, apologies and shaky make-ups
That never quite erase the dirt.

Feelings lurk like hungry ghosts:
Jealousy and spite at ex's posts,
Shame for folly on our part,
Anger we were duped or dropped,
Guilt for rashness with our heart.

Despite blameless self-deception,
If we recoil when love is lost
And chide ourselves for what it cost
With judgments taught in our past,
This strategy of self-protection
Thwarts finding partners who will last.

Although thinking we've moved on,
Resentment savored for too long
Hides the trauma unforgiven
That keeps us safe but still in prison.

When victim memories won't let go
And we don't comfort our distress,
Life and past remain in limbo...
But when self-compassion mends our pain,
Our heart is freed to love again.

By Darlene Lancer

Regretting Regrets

Those were summers lost raining tears,
Composing romance in thin air,
Waiting and pining for listless years,
Hunting for clues, comparing to her.

What went wrong that was rebuffed?
Grief without closure.
Why without answer.
They loved, but didn't love enough.

Potent daybreaks came and went.
Willing suitors stood in the wing.
Untold pleasures never spent.
Looking backward brought nothing.

A folly wasting so much life,
Wallowing in "What if's or was"
No doubt, because, it kept me safe
Though they moved on.
I'm regretting regrets
For years bygone.

RELATIONSHIPS

Exchanging pain for love,
Sorrow for joy,
Not knowing how to live.
No time to squander or to weep.
Now, it's me I must forgive
Before the endless sleep.

By Darlene Lancer

Without You

You told me I couldn't.
You told me I wouldn't do anything without you.
It was tough. The first drags of fresh air stung my lungs.
The sunlight was too bright.
The ground beneath my feet swayed like a pendulum.
I couldn't I wouldn't do anything without you.

Then I clasped hold of life.
Its beauty shone.
It told me I could, it told me I would do it all without you.

Some days were long.
Some nights waited as I held my breath for the dawn.
I lost my way on the path often.
But I remembered that I would, that I could,
Do it without you.

There are many miles between us now.
Your memory is still tangled in the gorse bushes around me,
And I stumble when I remember, your voice so clear in my ear:
I couldn't, I wouldn't live without you.

But there is beauty.
It's in the days of freedom and the nights of rest.
It's in the sun as it rises and the birdsong as I listen.
It catches my breath and it holds me close.

It paints the sky with a rainbow and says look where you are!

You said I couldn't, you said I wouldn't
Do anything without you.
But look at the sky. Hear the birdsong.
Do you notice the message written for you?

My life is beginning. My days are brightening.

So, I hope you can do your all without me.

By Suzanne Henderson
Author of *Life's Path*

The Gibson Player

Expectantly, at six, I welcome Lee.
"I'm on time," he crows, so trustworthy.

We dine, recline, and stretch our feet
Across my coffee table.
"It's too bright in here," he claims.
So 'round his toes I veer
to switch from lamp to candlelight.

While Lee plucks the Gibson on his knee.
Jasmine scent perfumes the spell.
He strums and croons and brags to me
He once played for Joni Mitchell.

With conscious touch he tours my hand,
His—rough from pitching ball today.
I nestle in his teal knit shirt,
Which compliments his grey.
"You melt my heart," he sighs
And puts my palm across his chest.

My mind is fraught with hope he's not,
And fears he's like the rest.
I gaze into his hazel eyes that gleam of life and wit,
"You're beautiful, " he adds without a blink.

RELATIONSHIPS

In frantic search of words,
I won't admit I'm trembling on the brink—
I want to kiss (He's tried on every date),
But think his kiss will lead to tears,
So in the amber glow we wait.

By Darlene Lancer

Awakening

After all the years of waiting,
Now when you come calling,
Tears not shed in solitude
Surprisingly are falling.

I want to draw you close to me,
But my heart is sorely broken
From the many loves before
Who left me at the door.

How can I trust foolishly
You won't do the same?
There is no guarantee
When love calls unexpectedly.

Who you are I can't distinguish
From my aching wish and fantasy
To fill my heart's emptiness
And set its passion free.

Guarded in an unseen prison,
Life passes safely by my cell.
Unsure this time love freely given
Can wake me from my sleeping spell.

RELATIONSHIPS

Now, in late December,
No hot flame to flare and spark,
But a slowly glowing ember
Ignites my long-sequestered heart.

A trampled rose lies in the grass,
Weak like mended glass,
For barren years too frail to stand.
In hope that love will cleanse my tears,
I dare to offer you my hand
And slowly rise to love again.

By Darlene Lancer

Beneath the Mask

When our heroes all have died
And the truth we finally know,
Will we love the fools inside,
Not raising them above,
Nor casting them below?

Will we disdain the men we hail,
Without a cloak of manliness?
When we see them flawed and frail,
Can we love them nonetheless?

When women claim their liberty,
Will men praise their female power
And admit their own dependency,
Abandoning their fort and tower?

When our ideal slips and stumbles,
Whom we depend on to be strong,
Can we see a child that fumbles
Or will we make them wrong?

Can we lift the mask of shame
That keeps us from each other,
And love the self we hide in vain
From our sister and our brother?

RELATIONSHIPS

Pleaser, sinner, bully, sage,
Get the actors off the stage,
Rebel, victim, saint, and scholar,
"Stop the play!" someone holler.

Can we put our shame aside
And forego the roles we play,
Disrobing fear dressed up as pride,
Our judgments dropping by the way.

Strip down the personality,
And look through others' eyes.
Beneath the make-up, you will see
Yourself revealed without disguise.

Can we let our heroes die
And face the truth and not the lie,
Can we love in all directions
When we take back our projections?

When will we end this masquerade
And see on close inspection,
Our ego has been too afraid
To see our own reflection?

So peak inside the mirror now,
It's our shadow we must face.
For if we want to love each other,
It's ourselves we must embrace.

UNFETTERED SOUL

No one better, no one worse,
No rank above, nor caste below,
We're all unique, yet all the same,
Equality we'll one day know.

By Darlene Lancer

When Talking's Better than Sex

For months on end we talked past three,
I loved to watch him think.
He told me his philosophy,
And I acted like his shrink.

He'd place his hand along my thighs,
While I listened to him mesmerized.
His words flowed into me,
Each thought ascending higher.

Our minds attuned in harmony,
Our hearts burned with desire.
In every field we shared our views.
Then by way of illustration,
He kissed me and our passion fused,
Mounting our frustration.

Erotic turned the conversation,
My pussy getting wet.
When finally yielding to sensation,
The mind fuck beat the sex.

By Darlene Lancer

Lessons Beyond the Body

You taught us about spirit.
You lit the way where we feared go,
And grasped what we could not imagine.

When you struggled,
You gave us laughter.

When you stumbled,
You taught us honesty.

When you were afraid,
You taught us courage.

When you couldn't walk,
You gave us strength.

When you suffered,
You taught us compassion.

When you needed help,
You taught us humility.

When you couldn't eat,
You gave us nourishment.

When you couldn't speak,
You gave us love.

RELATIONSHIPS

When you couldn't breathe,
You gave us inspiration.

When there was no hope,
You taught us faith.

We never thought you'd leave us,
But when you did,
You left your light.

By Darlene Lancer
Kay Hudson died at 54 of ALS in 1998

Contemplation

Even before we enter the world, our brains and hormones are wired for connection. Our first relationship begins in our mother's womb, where we recognize her voice and respond to her moods through hormones and stress responses. Later, her smell and touch become familiar. Affection and responsive communication are necessary for our brains and bodies to fully develop.

Early interactions with our parents shape our self-image and template for love and relationships, examined in "Mother Wounds." Our patterns of relating and reacting, our attachment style, are often repeated in adult relationships—romantic and otherwise—as explored in "Winter" and "The Gordian Knot."

A secure attachment in an intimate relationship can empower, enliven, and uplift us. It celebrates our successes and comforts us in defeat and sorrow. However, despite these potential benefits, many of us have had painful romantic relationships, and some have never truly known a safe one. Without consistent, unconditional love from *both* parents, we may confuse love with pain and longing, leading to feelings of being smothered, controlled, or rejected.

Love can be fickle. Even when we know better, we can be drawn to someone who causes us pain, as illustrated in several poems. We cannot make someone return our love nor make ourselves love the person who might be the best choice! Yet, we do have an option to walk away, as painful as that might be. Often the most difficult relationships serve as our greatest teachers, as was true in "Mental Chess," "Lost in Eden," and "Lady Anxiety."

How often do we idealize love, believing it will redeem our shame and alleviate our unhappiness? This illusion is poignantly captured in "The Cost of Love." Romantic love feels easy and exhilarating, bringing joy and passion, but it's temporary and doesn't equate to true love. When a romance ends, it can be heartbreaking because passions are at their peak and we're still in the idealization stage. Breakups bring grief that takes its toll on our vitality and our self-esteem, described in "Regretting Regrets." In codependent relationships, the loss of a partner may illuminate how we've lost ourselves, making recovery a vital journey of self-reclamation, beautifully depicted in "Lost in Eden" and "Without You."

Progressing from romantic infatuation to mature love is no easy task. Rainer Rilke wrote, *"For one human being to love another: that is perhaps the most difficult of all our tasks."* When we no longer try to impress our partner, eventually conflicting needs and differences surface. Love heightens our sensitivities. Separations and small discrepancies become magnified, distressing us. We feel disappointed and betrayed when our partner doesn't behave how they did initially nor according to our ideal expectations.

Eventually, one partner dominates or both engage in power struggles to assert their needs. However, we don't see our partner clearly, as mentioned in "Awakening." Our mind clouds our perception with idealization and positive or negative filters. Each relationship involves at least six people, including two sets of parents, whose behavior and beliefs lurk in the background until we become conscious of them. Relationships provide a mirror to these hidden aspects of our personality—our shadow. Our wounds are exposed.

Self-esteem is predictive of relationship satisfaction, but shame, and the associated trauma, is love's executioner because it creates insecurity and lack of self-worth. It can manifest in cycles of disconnection and barriers to intimacy that prevent closeness and honesty. Intimacy inevitably triggers aspects of our earliest close relationships, including prior hurts and childhood trauma, heightening our anxiety and fear of rejection (referred to in "The Gibson Player" and "Awakening.") When we fail to accept ourselves, we may discount our loved ones.

Through projection, we attribute the cause of our unhealed hurt, trauma, and shame to the other person. In so doing, we unknowingly judge aspects of our partner that we dislike in ourselves or our parents, assuming our partner is the source of our hurt. Because shame distorts our self-image, we also see it reflected to us in our partner's eyes. Then we react defensively to what we imagine, fueling destructive cycles that perpetuate past relational trauma. This creates an endless loop where our reactions are rooted in past wounds rather than the present reality. The more we are unconscious of them, the less choice we have over whom we love and our reactions. Without shame, we would not accept our partner's criticisms as valid and would set healthy boundaries.

To endure and grow, partnerships require maturity, independence, respect, sacrifice, and commitment. We must become skilled in empathy, acceptance, and compromise. As noted by Erich Fromm, immature love says, *"I love you because I need you,"* whereas mature love says, *"I need you because I love you."* Mature love is based on interdependence, not neediness. It's a vulnerable decision to depend on someone who has earned our trust.

Mindful relationships offer a path toward wholeness and increased humanity. Our projections and discomfort with one another's differences present opportunities for transformation. Yet, we must feel safe enough to communicate openly, lovable enough to receive love, and secure enough to give it freely. Both giving and receiving love present additional pitfalls. Love challenges us to recognize and lower our defenses to allow for vulnerability and authentic communication. In baring our soul, parts of ourselves are revealed that we may not even recognize. Healing enables us to make informed choices about our values and behavior, improving our relationships and facilitating personal growth and individuation.

Self-awareness places accountability on ourselves. By exploring the seeds of our attitudes and painful reactions, we can listen non-defensively and observe the strengths, limitations, and opinions of others. With greater objectivity, we can "take back our projections," suggested in "Beneath the Mask."

Whatever irritates us about our partner and others can lead us to greater self-knowledge. But it's not only our unpleasant traits we project. In idealizing our partner we may be denying and projecting our untapped strengths, discipline, talent, courage, and creativity. This process enhances love and empathy for others and ourselves. Through divine alchemy, by revealing our true self and navigating love's obstacles, in healing relationships intimacy and acceptance of our partner and ourselves deepen.

Relationships, even brief ones—especially those that open our hearts—leave an imprint on our soul, noted in the elegy, "Lessons Beyond the Body." We remain connected and shaped by shared memories, feelings, and experiences. While life is a deeply subjective journey, our intertwined narratives influence and define us. Embracing the interplay between ourselves and others helps to release the illusion of objectivity and accept the emotional truth of our connections. Though we may heal from past wounds, we are indelibly touched by our encounters, each one a lesson in love and self-discovery.

ANGST

Tomorrow

Green buds coming up
Too slow, I thought,
Will they grow?
I don't know, perhaps they'll die.

The stems are barren, just a leaf or two;
Some are sickly with white fly.
Another vine looks even worse,
No leaves at all, just tips of green.

This one has no chance, I judged,
while gazing at the light green buds.
A soft voice whispered: "Patience, wait and see."
No, I can't believe.

I need proof right now this plant will grow,
I'm too afraid, I cannot wait
For what tomorrow brings.
Black is all I see.
I cannot trust, nor can I hope,
For then who would I be?

By Darlene Lancer

Thin Armor

I have a coat of thin armor
It's shattered by now,
Worn down by life's blows,
Yet, it covers me somehow.

My armor will shield me
From sorrow and pain.
I need to use it
Again and again.
It covers me somehow.

My thin suit of armor
Will let me regain
The strength and the power
That keeps me so sane.

This sheath of thin armor
Keeps hurt away.
It covers me when
I abhor what they say.

You can hear their insanity.
It's muffled but loud.
And the damn thin armor
Seems no more than a shroud.

UNFETTERED SOUL

The world is spinning.
It's out of control.
But I've got this armor
And it protects me...
Sometimes, somehow.

It covers me,
Somehow.
Yes, it covers me,
S o m e h o w...

By Mike Gormley
Found on music platforms by jackiO

Forced Altruism

To make you feel good, I was:
Deliberately dropping the pot.
The world's biggest clown.
Talking about my worst blunders.
Poorly parallel parking the car on purpose,

To feel good,
I distance myself from the one who knows all my mistakes,
And will use them against me.

By Ole Kevin Rodberg

Canyons

Walled chambers of my mind guard the waterways of life.
Forever watching river rafts
And passersby floating in their gaiety,
I walk along the banks staring out as life goes by,
Endlessly watching from the distant shore.

Unable to hear the silent laughter,
Unable to see but a few feet ahead,
Unable to touch their smiling faces,
Unnoticed, I make my way
Through canyons that surround me.

There was a time when I had dreams,
When I had plans and hopes and schemes,
They mean nothing to me now.
Just endless waiting in vast empty canyons,
I can't see out of or through.

By Darlene Lancer

Desert Soul

Late November, I've been walking in the desert of my soul
Along the dry, uncertain bedrock of a once lively stream.
A stream that sparkled and moved swiftly, with assurance,
That clamored over rocks and broken trees,
Racing to some mindless destination.

Until Spring, when floods came to kill a child at play
And rip away the chiseled outline of the riverbed.

I step cautiously not to falter on silent stones uncovered,
Wandering lost in the vast, unchartered,
Long-forgotten emptiness left behind.
I find a crooked path that takes me where I do not know.
Little strength to move on, I stop frequently to rest.

A white-tailed rabbit running in the brush
Rouses my delight and wonder.
He stops and listens for direction, then vanishes in the dust.
Leaving me to meander the riverbed of my life.

By Darlene Lancer

My Violin

I had a violin that sang so sweet.
But was damaged in the wars,
Abused by careless players,
I found it battered on the floor.

Weeping, I rocked it like a dying child,
Wrapped it in raw silk
To keep it safe from hands and soil.

Too fragile to play, I locked it in my cabinet,
But could see it through the glass.
Life came and went, and day by day,
I failed to glance it when I passed,
And soon forgot my broken violin.

By Darlene Lancer

I Want to Flow Away

The further I delve into you,
The further away from myself I become.
I want to flow away,
Tear myself apart,
Find out what's inside.
Let it pour out.

I looked in the mirror.
Looked down.
Didn't want him to see.
That I've made him so small,
So small,
That there is nothing left.

By Ole Kevin Rodberg

Shame

What does it mean when I want to hide,
Find a corner, cower, and let it pass?
In the silent dark I take my chide,
So that I may re-join the mass.

I so want to be a good man,
I'd give my soul for so to be,
Quell the fear and draw the calm,
From myself no longer flee.

I fear the dark and lonely places,
I've seen the scars they leave behind.
Even in the light, and with familiar faces,
I remain within the shadows of my mind.

I don't believe I'm such a bad man,
Far from perfect, that's for sure,
But feelings rise that I'm but a sham,
Despite those efforts to reassure.

Of all my pains and source of harrow,
None pricks my worth as much,
Than being the source of someone's sorrow,
And reparation beyond my clutch.

ANGST

Perhaps I am a lost man,
A cast aside and damaged good,
Maybe grand such was the plan,
Signed and sealed from early childhood.

I should and do show gratitude,
For the bounty I was bestowed,
But worth of being does me elude,
For in the worth of others my seed was sowed.

By Owen Reynolds

Initiation at Karabel's Dancewear

I cover my toes with white lamb's wool,
And slip on pink satin toe shoes.
At last my own!
I wrap 'round my ankles
Pink satin ribbon,
Crisscross, tie, and tuck in place.

Years of échappes and pirouettes,
Dancing Swan Lake's *Love Duet*.
I watch pros rub battered, bleeding feet
And don their broken, tattered shoes
In dressing rooms moist with dancers' sweat.

I long for arches leaning over toes,
But on point, my feet soon ache,
Too flat and weak to break the inner soles
And wear away those satin toes,
That mark the ballerina I'll never be.

By Darlene Lancer

Waiting

Waiting. Waiting for life to begin.
Waiting for love to come in.
Frozen in time.
Tic, Tic, Tic.

Life is vast. Life is bold.
Life is wild.
Tic, Tic.

Immovable walls surround me.
A gale slams against my door.
Obscurely, healing crawls with dubiety,
While entropy grinds on.
Tic.

Destruction silently lurks.
A virus, the wind, a word, an accident
Break me while I sit waiting.
Death does not wait.
I cannot wait.

By Darlene Lancer

Letting Go

How do you soothe a heart that yearns
And forget unlived dreams it keeps?
How do you discard what you never had
While death crawls silently in sleep.

When the future holds uncertainty,
How do you heal the seeds you've sown,
With no hope to soothe the pain
While wishing for what can't be grown?
Need and longing still remain,
Ever tied to Sisyphus' stone.

How do you pause the snow birds' flight
Or a praying mantis mating?
How can you keep moths from the light
Or the Great Migration waiting?

It's hard to accept what never was,
Fruitless searching for the prize,
While ignoring the hungry child inside,
In stillness, love and peace abide.

By Darlene Lancer

Contemplation

Many of us live with worry and discontent that has become so familiar that we don't recognize it as anxiety or depression until some uninvited event immobilizes us. Our distress is often caused by distorted thinking, described in "Tomorrow" and "Perfection" in the section on Perspective. The culprit is generally shame, which breeds fear and anguish, or a real or anticipated loss—whether it's a relationship ending, a decline in our resources or abilities, or the fading of unfulfilled dreams. We may feel adrift and unable to grapple with a reality that seems heavy and unyielding. Acceptance doesn't come easily; it demands we face our grief and embrace our past mistakes.

Yet, when childhood trauma lingers in the shadows, it complicates our journey, hindering our capacity to move forward. As depicted in "Thin Armor" and "Forced Altruism," we may develop self-protective defenses to hide our anxiety, shame, and depression. Learned coping mechanisms are usually useless to deal with life's painful lessons. If we were overly indulged in childhood, our needs not met, or our disappointment not consoled, we can become easily discouraged, withdraw, and fall into depression. Beneath these struggles lies the emptiness of a child whose parents didn't understand or give help, described in "Canyons" and "Desert Soul."

Failure to heal past wounds contributes to depression and may lead to re-traumatization, creating a cycle of cascading trauma. This is reflected in *My Violin*, where the failure to heal keeps us trapped in sorrow. Sometimes, we aren't even aware of the root cause of our grief, indicating a refusal to let go and move forward from what we've lost. This refusal to mourn makes us more vulnerable to recurring self-perpetuating bouts of depression, leading to paralysis and isolation.

While loss is painful, depression may be caused and exacerbated by self-pity or self-recriminations, creating further guilt and shame. This is explored in "I Want to Flow Away" and "Shame." We can become mired in self-blame, which deepens our emotional distress.

Growing up inevitably involves loss and disappointment, as reflected in "At Karabel's Dancewear." Mourning is an important step in recovery. Clinging to the past or unattainable dreams, blaming ourselves or others, or resisting the reality of what is can entrench us in prolonged depression. Freud noted that melancholia stems from an unwillingness to mourn. By fixating on past losses and missed opportunities, we allow sadness to linger indefinitely, overshadowing our present and future possibilities.

Life presents us with thorns and roses. Our happiness depends on where we place our attention. Circular thinking, feeling victimized by fate, or waiting for events to change, as depicted in "Waiting," blind us from real solutions and obstruct finding happiness and gratitude in what life offers.

Healing and maturity allow us to shed our illusions, accept reality, and take proactive steps to meet our needs. We may feel hopeless, but our condition is not hopeless. Perceived hopelessness often results from negative thinking that obscures the possibility of change. Changing our attitude changes everything.

I experienced a period of depression while on crutches for several years. One day at the YMCA, I met a woman who had only one leg but was full of vitality after swimming. I complimented her courage and asked if she ever felt depressed. She seemed surprised and replied, "Fortunately, no, except for the first six months. I just love to swim." Her acceptance of her circumstances and pursuit of joy despite them were inspiring. By getting support to take unprecedented risks, eventually, I'd be climbing a mountain.

Finding purpose in our pain can also alleviate what may feel like senseless misery. Self-inquiry about what we learned, how we have changed, and whether we're intolerant and self-righteous of ourselves or others can provide strength and hope to avoid repeating past mistakes.

Instead of remaining passive victims living in our past, *action* is what is needed—engaging in new interests and activities. Not all solutions depend on us. We need support from a therapist, coach, our family, or 12-step or other support group to persevere and keep moving forward. Reaching out for help, exercising, socializing, pampering yourself, and pursuing creativity are essential.

Often great difficulties precede enlightenment. When things look bleakest, it's an invitation to delve deeper, nurture ourselves, and connect with our spirituality, knowing that feelings are only feelings and that they too shall pass. The Buddhist saying, "The sun is always shining," reminds us that despite the clouds and rain, when we rise above them, we see more clearly that God is there and our true self is unharmed.

When all seems lost, when our hopes and dreams dissolve, we are forced to surrender to what is—to "Let go, and let God." It's not easy as described in "Letting Go," nor a one-time act, but a repeated practice. Ultimately, by embracing our pain and seeking support, we can transform despair into resilience.

CHANGE AND TRANSFORMATION

Familiar Safety

A neighbor's cat liked to dally
Along the far side of the alley.
Unaware, I sped in his direction,
And, though safely out of harm,
He turned, alarmed, and for protection,
Quickly scrammed to his back door.
I slammed my brakes to the floor.

Kitty's refuge lay beyond his ken.
I thought how like the cat are we.
Although it risks our jeopardy,
When peril threatens, we rush "home,"
Seeking safety in our patterns known.

By Darlene Lancer

Courage

Courage is the earnest prayer
That tames a fretful mind,
Courage is the pain we bear
When hope is left behind.

Courage speaks in honesty,
Though loss may surely follow,
Truth bends the will reluctantly
To chance what lies tomorrow.

And courage will in silence wait,
Though design would intercede,
And instead allows the hand of fate
Its tapestry to weave.

Courageous is the pioneer,
Who takes the obscure roads,
Not resting in the known and clear,
But lives as life unfolds.

Courage is the willingness
To unveil the shadow of our being,
And face the fear, the grief, and emptiness
that give life authentic meaning.

UNFETTERED SOUL

Courage bids, "Surrender pride
look behind the mirror,"
To embrace, not shame, the flaws inside,
And make amends for error.

Courage doesn't walk away
From darkness in its path,
But meets the night assailing day,
With truth, and love and wrath.

Courage is the heart unsealed,
Though temptation is to hide,
Courage is the soul revealed,
All armor set aside.

Courage lives reality,
Each moment full and clear,
With patience and integrity,
The path to strength from fear.

By Darlene Lancer

The Caterpillar

Hello, furry creature,
Wriggling through blades of grass.
I reach to hold you in my hand,
But quick you curl and close,
Then, wait and wait before you crawl again.

No word, nor touch can speed your trust,
But by and by, once more you try.
Through dirt and leaves you make your way,
Until one day you coil and die,
Not knowing if, nor how, nor when,
You wake, reborn a butterfly.

By Darlene Lancer

River of Time

An unsung song beckons to me,
On billowing mists flowing in from the sea,
Whispering shards of my soul's lost dream
And bittersweet days wrapped in memory.

Fog obscures what tomorrows bring.
No longer racing through alleys blind,
Learning to wait for the sun to climb,
Listening for words to a song I'll sing,
I quietly rest in the river of time.

By Darlene Lancer

The Tale They Told

It was never meant to be like this, they said.
We're so sorry, they said.

But they were wrong.
For it was always meant to be like this.

The struggle,
Like a thousand birds beating their wings
Against the cage of her heart.

The despair,
Like the darkest night settling
Over all of her world.

The misery,
Like stones weighting her down
Until she sank.

But they forgot to mention
The best part,

The part where
The birds escaped,
Her heart opening like a rose.

And the morning came
When she saw the light

UNFETTERED SOUL

And the weightlessness
As she rose
Resplendent
Into who she was.

For they were wrong all along.
It was always meant to be like this.

And she was glad.

By Suzanne Henderson
Author of *Life's Path*

Beautiful Dreamer

I laid down my book to play piano
One afternoon in '82,
And fingered "Beautiful Dreamer,"
As my father used to do.

No words, no understanding,
Tears streaming down my face—
Unaware of why, in a dream myself,
Drawn by a force unknown.

It was I,
Awakening from slumber,
From the life I'd lived asleep,
Not my own.
Soon I'd leave my marriage, my children,
My profession, and my home.

By Darlene Lancer

The 4th of July

Dreaming I was fishing,
I drew a snake up from the depths.
It wriggled on the ground.
The hook popped out its mouth
As it whipped around.

Afraid, I grabbed its neck
And called for help. No one came.
I squeezed with all my strength,
As poison sprayed from its fangs.
The snake's strong back turned limp and lifeless in my hand,
And I felt power.

By Darlene Lancer

The Engagement Ring

A solitaire danced above
A swirl of twirling light,
Radiating timeless love,
Promised by my shining knight.
Diamonds blazed in each direction.
For me, she was, like him, perfection.

I wore my ring around the clock.
Washed ten thousand times.
Daily it was knocked and jarred.
Platinum prongs were loose and marred.

Baby diamonds disappeared.
Each one I grieved in despair,
Though stronger it became,
Repair upon repair.

Bit by bit it dimmed and changed.
New diamonds mixed with old.
Through the years its value waned–
Prongs soldered with white gold.

UNFETTERED SOUL

Too delicate for life,
It scratched while exercising.
I often hid my ring away.
Unfettered, I ceased compromising,
And finally took it off to stay.

By Darlene Lancer

The Red Kimono

I sipped morning tea,
Wrapped in my red kimono
With embroidered peach blossoms
Near a gold and green teahouse.
Luxurious, soft, smooth cotton kept me cool in summer,
Warm in winter.

Hank gave me many fine gifts,
But this was my favorite.
Prized for its wash and wear ability,
Its sleeves cleared the kitchen sink for chores.

Deep, decorated pockets held daily necessities:
Kleenex, a nail file, jewelry.
Comforting, breezy cloth nourished skin thirsty for oxygen.
Yoga was easy in its spacious fluidity.

After years, the shoulder seams unraveled. I sewed them up.
Its pockets opened holes; no longer safe. I mended them.
Side seams frayed. I sewed them, too.
Stitches loosened like an epidemic.
Still, I mended it.

UNFETTERED SOUL

Finally, light showed through the gauze
Where seat threads wore thin.
It couldn't be saved. Was I careless? At fault for laundering it?
I never wanted to part with my beautiful, red kimono.

Decades passed.
Then one day, without reflection, I put it in the trash.

By Darlene Lancer

Contemplation

Growing up, I'd heard a variation of Aristotle's adage, *"Give me a child until he is 7, and I will show you the man."* At my first 12-step meeting, I received a glimmer of hope upon listening to people share how much they'd changed; yet, I wondered if I could.

Depression often signals a need for change, but, changing isn't easy and transitions can be daunting, especially when we're letting go of the old while facing an uncertain future. It's natural to resist making change and usually focus on the risks and downside before we can see the benefits. We fill the unknown with potential obstacles and negative projections, including anticipated failure. In truth, we're mostly afraid of our own self-judgment.

There also is a sense of security in "the devil we know." As creatures of habit, we often cling to familiar patterns, much like worn-out shoes that no longer provide support. Especially, when we experience stress or adversity, we easily revert to our defensive habits, even if they no longer serve us. Fear can paralyze us, limiting our perspective and blinding us to alternative solutions, ultimately, exposing us to greater harm, as depicted in "Familiar Safety."

However, nothing remains the same forever. Permanence is an illusion; change is inevitable. Life is in constant flux. We, too, are part of this ever-changing process. To grow and mature, we must adapt accordingly.

Often pain signals that our lives are misaligned with our true self, urging us to grow, change, heal, and pursue new opportunities. However, new doors won't open until we close the old ones behind us. This process may require the awareness to alter our plans and beliefs, the motivation to acquire new skills, and the grief to let go of relationships and dreams we hold dear, as expressed in "Letting Go" in the previous section.

Change marks growth, but requires courage, as Maya Angelou wrote, "...*without courage, you can't practice any other virtue consistently.*" Courage manifests in many forms, as examined in "Courage." Most of us need support and guidance to navigate change, especially when the stakes feel high, unpredictable, and beyond our control. Much like the butterfly, a symbol of transformation, emerging from its cocoon, we have no prior conception of the healing and heights we can reach, as described in "The Caterpillar."

We may seek transformation, but living intentionally in alignment with our principles and objectives requires a conscious commitment. Recovery involves changing our attitudes and behaviors, accepting responsibility for our problems and our happiness, and initiating thoughtful action. This demands courage and honesty to examine ourselves, our behavior, painful emotions, and buried memories—particularly daunting when we have a shame-based view of ourselves, we're afraid of uncovering and exposing our perceived inadequacies.

CHANGE AND TRANSFORMATION

Building strength and confidence through this process can be difficult for codependents who have lived passively reacting to others or waiting for them to change. But when our pain outweighs our fear of change, we're motivated to take the necessary steps to transform our lives. The Serenity Prayer offers valuable guidance: *"God grant me the serenity to accept the things we cannot change, the courage to change the things we can, and the wisdom to know the difference."* While we may still have fear, this prayer encourages us to relinquish control and take action. By changing what we can—ourselves—our relationships improve. On the other hand, sometimes wisdom instructs us that patience is needed. It takes courage and faith to resist acting and wait, as depicted in "The River of Time."

Many of our patterns and coping mechanisms stem from growing up in a dysfunctional family, childhood trauma, or behaviors learned from parental figures. Embracing authenticity, setting boundaries, assertively expressing our feelings, wants, and needs expose our vulnerability to shame or abandonment. We may have to emotionally and physically distance ourselves from friends and family who don't support our strengths, as implied in "The Tale They Told." All these steps require considerable courage and often the guidance and support of an experienced coach, sponsor, or therapist.

When we feel overwhelmed, in crisis, or discouraged, it takes courage to get through the day, adhere to our principles, and maintain self-care without succumbing to self-pity, self-destructive habits, or hopelessness. When we inevitably slip, it takes strength to pick ourselves up and make renewed effort once more. We need courage in the face of disappointment, crises, and problems. While troubles are unavoidable, how we handle them presents growth opportunities.

Change may be foreshadowed in our impulses, described in "Beautiful Dreamer," or in dreams symbolizing transformation, as in the one on "The 4th of July," where I embrace my power to tame unconscious fears. The heart is slower to adapt. Often inner conflict arises when we recognize a need to change and are willing but are still unable to align our will with our feelings and actions. Failed attempts are frustrating; our will avails us nothing.

If we can let go, our unconscious evolves in response to our awareness of our powerlessness when greeted by patience and loving-kindness toward ourselves, not merely intellectually, but viscerally, in our body and feelings. Change occurs one day without much forethought. It happens through us, not directed by our ego or will, as exemplified in "The Engagement Ring" and "The Red Kimono."

A meditation practice cultivates patience, self-awareness, and equanimity. We're better prepared to face an uncertain future and gain the ability to reflect on our choices before we act. Prayers for courage and guidance can be powerful. We can simply ask for the courage to act in accordance with our highest good, for our higher power to walk beside us, and to guide our words and actions. While change may seem formidable, it's more manageable with faith and support, ultimately offering us opportunities for profound growth.

FAITH

The Monarch

On a windowsill a Monarch prays,
Stoic and still.
Motionless, near death it seems.
As cold winds beat its fragile wings.

I coax its hairy limbs to climb
Upon my waiting finger.
Life greets life, and eons vanish
As it finds a trust greater than its fright.

What alien hand will reach through time
To spare me from the cold dark night?
And will I know that help is mine,
or wait, half-frozen, for the light?

By Darlene Lancer

Gnarly

When I see weeds pierce cracked cement,
Or roots gnarl through pipes and walls,
I remember God's radiance can also crack
Cemented, gnarly patterns of my mind.

I need only sit and wait in faith that
Light will come not by me, but through me.

By Darlene Lancer

Colour

Red was the colour of my fear,
While white light changed my sky to bright,
Striped pink ribbon, to my delight.
Grey was the colour as dark days loomed,
And I shaded with heavy stroke
As the sky turned to a deep black night.

The blue decline of moody days
helped me see more colour bloom.
But soon yellow lit my sky with joy
When I saw the dawn break forth.

Green was the flourishing of my dreams.
A garden blooming with joy sublime.
The flowers grew from dirty soil, rainy days,
And sun at dawn.

People walk onto my stage.
They glow with light or fall from sight.
I embrace the colour of warmth,
Like a fire burning on the coldest days.

I follow His light as He shows me the way.
He paints the brightest picture of the world He loves.
The detailed touch of a creator great
Makes my eyes grow wide with awe.

FAITH

And when the flowers in my garden fade,
When dark clouds hide the views sublime,
When weeds grow and choke my hope,
I go to Him and ask for help.

Then the greatest painter ever known,
Paints my sky with hope and joy.
The birds sing in wonder at the sight,
And once again my world is bright.

By Suzanne Henderson
Author of *Life's Path*

Dreams and Distractions

Take me sailing, true Spirit,
On the ocean of Light.
My ship: joy, hope, and love.
My crew, all of you.

Where is this little ship bound in my mind?
Off into Dreamland? There what will I find?
A rare seed to plant to grow into bloom?
An unexplored corner of an interior room?

Or is it bound aimlessly into the dark?
Blown into enchantment that quenches the spark,
And buries my will beneath sweet distraction,
Steals my time, to my feet gives no traction?

Since I captain this ship of temptation,
It's me who charts its true North destination.
As I steady my hand with joy at the helm,
God's will is my guide through this curious realm.

By Ann Fuller

Surrender

Surrender is nothing one can *do*.
It's an absence I can't create.
It's what I must remove:

All that I want,
All that I understand,
All that I believe I am,
All that I hope for.
Then I surrender,
Not by choice, not easily.

If I abandon everything to find God,
That desire is still something.
I haven't let go.

In stillness, I surrender
The full and empty mind
That fills my heart with peace.
From each moment to the next
Abiding presence is all there is.
Surrender creeps in unnoticed.
"Ah ha," I say,
And surrender flies away.

By Darlene Lancer

Contemplation

In childhood, I lost trust in my parents and traditional religion and have since struggled with understanding and embracing the complexities of faith. Faith implies reliance on something beyond our ordinary consciousness. People generally associate faith with religion and adherence to religious texts and doctrines. I often envied those with a devout religious faith, as it can provide great succor in times of distress.

Although interpretations vary, major religions define God through their texts. Theistic religions share themes of viewing God as an omnipotent, omniscient, benevolent creator. However, faith needn't rely on such definitions. It can stem from spiritual principles, personal experiences, a higher power, or the universe devoid of established teachings. Many newcomers to Twelve Step programs who have abandoned their religious beliefs choose to place their faith in the group or the program's principles.

Some people consider God to be remote and impersonal, as an omnipotent creator, existing outside of the universe. In contrast, pantheists believe God to be synonymous with the universe and nature, existing in everything. Followers of panpsychism view God as an evolving, dynamic, interconnected creative process. For people who experience God as their personal higher power, guide, and companion, that power can manifest through common beliefs and norms, connection with nature, our collective unconsciousness comprised of archetypes, themes, and symbols, or through personal mystical, unitive, or transcendent experiences.

Faith requires not only belief, but to be helpful, it usually involves forms of prayer, study, contemplation, meditation, and communal experiences. Like any skill, faith requires practice. Many of us may have distanced ourselves from prayer and spiritual practices, or learned to rely on ourselves, forgetting that we're not alone.

I was unaccustomed to prayer and meditation. Over the decades, my relationship with God has had its ups and downs. I sought books, beliefs, groups, and practices well-suited to me, which gradually evolved into meditating and doing yoga regularly. A daily practice deepens spirituality. It develops a reservoir of faith to sustain us during stressful times when fear can dominate. Cultivating faith eases life's difficulties, calms our worries and emotions, and counters our natural tendencies toward negativity and control.

When praying, we may be unaware that we're seeking control for specific outcomes. Fear, rather than faith, often fuels our worries about whether our desires will ever be fulfilled, resulting in barriers that prevent us from fully experiencing life. We may find ourselves caught in a cycle of anxiety, holding back from pursuing our passions and dreams. In contrast, faith embraces uncertainty and welcomes unknowable possibilities. It opens our hearts to the present, allowing us to connect with the ever-changing aliveness of the moment and become receptive to help.

Much of our pain is self-inflicted and rooted in our attitudes and actions. We may not know what's best for us, and, as Shakespeare wrote, *"beg oft our harms."* Unwittingly, we might sabotage ourselves with self-fulfilling prophecies that reinforce negative beliefs.

Moreover, our brains are wired to focus on the negative, especially when conditioned to fear the unknown through parenting or repeated disappointment and painful experiences. Lacking faith and trust, we tend to expect the worst, as exemplified in "Tomorrow" in the section on Angst. However, this cognitive distortion causes needless suffering. It's a negative projection that blinds us to the bigger picture and ignores the possibility of positive outcomes. Faith encourages us to trust the process. It shifts our focus from negative to positive thoughts, reinforcing a more hopeful perspective that lifts our mood and energizes our relationships and endeavors.

Faith inherently implies humility, but many people aren't accustomed to asking for help. Pride often inhibits seeking assistance from a higher power and others. Or, our fear-driven ego and stubborn self-will seek to control and struggle against reality, preventing us from finding workable solutions.

Letting go of self-will is a challenge, especially for people in recovery. We want what we want when we want it! We become impatient and worry that our desire won't materialize. Acting on our fears can interfere with the natural unfolding of events. We may trigger other people's fear and defensiveness, making matters worse. Enabling or managing someone's life can prevent them from learning important lessons about taking responsibility for the consequences of their actions and self-reliance in finding solutions.

People unfamiliar with faith misunderstand humility and believe surrender implies a lack of action and power. However, admitting our powerlessness isn't resignation. It realigns our efforts and perspective and acknowledges the limits of our control, especially over other people. When we focus on our troubles, they increase. Embracing nonresistance and detachment brings peace and growth. Often we find new solutions or our problems resolve themselves. If not, we eventually learn to let go and better accept reality.

Life involves a continual process of letting go—whether it's of our desires, our youth, past experiences, or people who are no longer in our lives. At times, we must let go of unfulfilled hopes and dreams, as poignantly expressed in "Letting Go" in the previous section on Angst. This can be difficult, particularly letting go of negative emotions and beliefs.

When everything seems dark and overwhelming, instead of seeking known solutions, surrendering our problems by expressing our fear and pain and asking for help and guidance can provide peace and open us to unexpected answers. We learn to trust that things will work out as they are meant to, even if not always according to our plans, as mentioned in "The Tale They Told" in the section on Relationships. This radical shift in perspective benefits our lives and those around us.

Prayer is a way of communicating with our higher power. Prayer strengthens us and aligns our subconscious mind to work with us, not against us. Prayers of gratitude for what is good in our lives gradually shift our outlook and actions for the better. Various forms of meditation increase our awareness by calming the body and clearing the mind. Meditation and prayer connect us to ourselves and our source of strength. They loosen the ego's grip and encourage trust in inner guidance.

Practices like chanting and visualization can bypass the thinking mind, while observing nature can remind us of the universe's bountiful, creative power that inspired "Gnarly" and "Coleur." That same power streams through our cells if we don't block it with thoughts and emotions, as described in "Dreams and Distractions." By connecting to this unstoppable, overflowing, and eternal force, we can revitalize and heal ourselves, whether God is viewed as energy, a deity, or our higher self. As Jesus said, *"God is within."* There is a boundless source of energy both within us and all around us. By remaining open to this energy daily, we remind ourselves that we don't need to have all the answers.

Mindfulness meditation fosters greater self-awareness and creates distance between our thoughts and our reactions. It helps us stay present to experience reality as it is, unfiltered by our preconceptions. By quieting our mind, our preoccupations reveal our attitude toward life. Are we judgmental, worried, distracted, or striving for accomplishment? Our life reflects our attitudes. A peaceful mind promotes peace, worry breeds anxiety, and persistent striving creates strife.

FAITH

The highest form of prayer and meditation is to sit in silence. In letting go, we create a space where our soul is receptive to holy communion. As explored in "Surrender," we're challenged to completely let go and open our heart and mind to the present moment. The ability to overcome anxiety and distractibility while stilling the mind improves with practice. At first fleetingly, and later for longer periods, we notice the space between our breaths, thoughts, or the quiet of nature. When we experience consciousness without thought, we experience our timeless, true nature—beyond ego, conditioning, and form. In stillness, we can experience a deep sense of peace, unity, and profound love by connecting with the intrinsic energy that unites our experience with the fabric of all life.

The radiance of our creative life force allows divine alchemy to heal and transform us. It enlightens us to the truth, our unlived potential, and infinite possibilities. With practice, we become happier, calmer, and more accepting of people and the vicissitudes of life. New positive thoughts and ideas empower us to express ourselves, solve problems, and manifest our goals.

SELF-LOVE & HEALING

Life's Playground

Come play, said life...
Not today, I said.
Too much to do,
To say,
To mend.

So I said yes to strife.

To days that didn't stop,
To nights that wouldn't sleep,
And I forgot to breathe,
To laugh,
To sing.

Come play, said life....
How, I said. How?
When the chores don't stop,
And the bills pile up,
And the worry lines collect
Around my eyes,
How?

Let me show you, said Life...
Okay, I said with a sigh,
And I stepped away from the
Worries and the strife,
And I took a deep breath,
And I opened my arms.

Here I am, I said.
Show me life.
But hurry for I have chores to do!

Then life laughed for a while,
And the trees shook,
And the brooks trembled...
The world giggling along with her.

I didn't quite get the joke
And said I had to go.

Come play, said life...
When! I asked with a sigh.

Then the sky darkened
As life frowned,
And the thunder grumbled in disgust.

I fell to my knees as the whole world shook.

Now! Life cried, before it's too late.
And I looked down
And saw the cracks at my feet,
While the clock got louder,

And the sun dropped lower,
And lower,
Another day gone.

Come play, said life...
And then I knew.
And I ran from the chores
That would always wait.
And I ran from the worries
That were making me old.

Show me, I said....I'm ready now.
And I ran into the world
To see what I'd missed,
While I'd been busy making my plans.

All I can say is it's one big world.
There's mountains to climb,
And visions to see,
And so many places that my feet can explore.
There's people and places and so many things to see.
It's fun and exciting, and it's waiting for you!

Do you hear it now...there in the breeze?
That whisper to your heart?
It's time for you now!
It's time to live and explore and greet the people you meet.

UNFETTERED SOUL

Listen for life's cry...
Come out to play....

Don't wait.
Just go.

By Suzanne Henderson
Author of *Life's Path*

The One

You are the one I want to love
To be the smile that greets my heart
Who hears my secret dreams
And sees inside my soul.

You are the one I give delight,
Whose touch is tender in the night,
Whose holy passion knows no height.

You are the one whose voice I sing,
Whose words to me mean everything.
You are the one whose mind I yearn
To know and share the things we learn.

You make me laugh when I am sad
And promptly chide me when I'm bad.
You flirt and tease me when we play
And dazzle me with repartee.

You are there when I fall down.
You're my playmate when we clown.
You're the drumbeat of my heart
In rhythm near or far apart.

UNFETTERED SOUL

You are the one I've longed to love
Until the end of time.
The one I have been dreaming of,
Though a creation of my mind.

Confusing reality with what is not
And what I need with what I want.
A search for that I'll never find.
But can reveal within my Self,
The One who is divine.

By Darlene Lancer

Turnaround

Where are you going?
Where have you been?
Looking ever outward,
Looking deep within.
Leaving yourself behind.

Hoping for the future,
Digging in the past,
Seeking truth and explanations,
Finding answers do not last.

Now and then you stop to rest,
With worry and despair,
Asking others who know best,
Wanting lovers who will care.
Leaving yourself behind.

Imploring God for help divine
For guidance to be clear.
Your reasoning and thinking
So loud you cannot hear.

Holding on too tight
To listen and to know,
No room enough to breathe,
Nor time left to let go.

UNFETTERED SOUL

Neglected needs and buried dreams
Blanketed by shame,
Truth sacrificed for love,
Still failed to curb the pain.

Working so hard,
Your ego on stage,
Directing the show
With pride fueled by rage.

For decades you were floundering,
Believing you were strong,
Denying you were powerless,
Afraid of being wrong.

When did you turn left,
Instead of turning right?
A long, long time ago,
You faded out of sight.
Leaving yourself behind

Searching for the path,
That fateful intersection,
Forgetting who you are,
Losing your direction.

Up and down the road again
Attempting to reclaim,
Trying to remember when
You silently forgot your name.

SELF-LOVE & HEALING

You danced a tune for others' eyes
And sang for others' ears,
Slowly donning each new guise,
Your own voice waned through the years.
Leaving yourself behind.

Turnaround my love and look at me,
The answers you will find,
In the present you will see
The one you left behind.

Turn inward love, and listen,
Your own voice faint you'll hear,
The only one you longed to love
Was always waiting near.

By Darlene Lancer

I'll Be There

When life has lost its meaning,
And friends have turned away,
When your face is lined and hair is grey,
I'll be there for you.

When hope has flickered from your sight
And the candles have all burned out,
When nothing gets you through the night,
I'll be there for you.

After all the disappointments,
And all the tears are shed,
When everything's been tried and said,
I'll be there for you.

After plans and efforts all go wrong,
And tomorrow doesn't matter,
When you finally think you can't go on,
I'll be there for you.

When you've lost what you hold dear,
And have nothing left to give,
When you don't know if you want to live,
I'll be there for you.

When there's no reprieve from constant pain,
And no one understands,

SELF-LOVE & HEALING

When words are useless to explain,
I'll be there for you.

When finally you have shelved your dreams,
And after all the tears,
When life is worse than all your fears,
I'll be waiting there for you.

And when your strength and courage leave,
And no one else can help,
When there's nothing left you can believe,
I'll still be waiting there for you.

By Darlene Lancer

Soul Waters

I thought the ocean too cold to swim.
But dipped my hand slowly in.
Surprised to find the sun
Had warmed the Winter water.

How often do I hesitate,
Believing it's too cold,
Forgetting I can drop into
The warm, lush depths
That vitalize my soul.

By Darlene Lancer

On Being Strong

It's not the fight that sets things right.
It's not the bold expression.
It's the steady eye and gentle words
That follow firm intention.

I always envied eloquence –
Audacious words that squared the score.
But in my years, I have learned
Calm confidence conveys much more.

Strength and courage were my ambition,
Yet models I had few.
Might and nerve are only earned
By what we daily do.

By Darlene Lancer

Dear Heart

I asked my heart if it would open.
"Too risky," it replied.

Time is wasting, don't you see?
"No. Time means not a thing to me."

You sang when romance felt so splendid.
"But heartsick when the music ended."

Love can soothe the hurt you've known.
"And grief remains when love is gone."

Hope for love that lasts next time.
"Hope is foolish for the blind."

Why still cling to past and pain?
"Too oft I risked and lost again."

Can you leave the past behind?
"I'm in a mess. I can't unbind."

Your life now bids you to revive.
"In the dark I safely hide.
Or, perhaps ago I died inside."

SELF-LOVE & HEALING

You suppose that tears you bleed
Will open up your heart.
In truth they dredge the primal seed
That beset you from the start.

"How can I change, unlock love's door?
"I don't know how to trust once more."

Dear heart,
You need not hope nor trust to heal,
But share truthfully what you feel.

By Darlene Lancer

My Ship Comes Home

I'd been searching all my life,
Never knowing why,
Seeking answers without questions,
Afraid to live, afraid to die.

I looked worldwide, tried meditation,
Fueling my desire,
In books, in mind, found fascination,
Thinking I was climbing higher.

Sports and pleasures, men to love,
Yearning after each new goal,
Ecstatic highs to float above
Never soothed my restless soul.

In all the work I've tried and done,
My eyes were on my dreams,
Despite the praise, success and fun,
What's real was never what it seemed.

For many years I stayed asleep,
Dreaming through my life,
Living others' plans for me,
A daughter, lawyer, mother, wife.

SELF-LOVE & HEALING

On waking one day from my slumber
I found a wasteland all around.
So hard to crawl back out from under,
I began a journey homeward bound.

I lacked a ship to start my voyage.
No sails courageous or iron mast.
No map to chart my course unknown.
No rudder strong in trust steadfast.

Tidal waves would lie ahead
Of pain and grief and fear unseen,
My past arising from the dead,
The nightmare that was once the dream.

I looked for signs, but saw only darkness.
I had no compass for direction.
I'd sail, and drift, and sink again,
But winds of love were my protection.

I rode the waves, my boat capsizing,
Through a never ending stormy night.
Then gradually a dawn was rising,
Happiness was in my sight.

I found a love within my heart
And peace I'd never known.
After searching everywhere,
I learned my "Self" was always home.

By Darlene Lancer

Follow Your Dreams

Follow your dreams,
Don't let them die.
Let your heart lead you.
Don't ask why.
Wherever it takes you,
Just follow, follow, follow.

You are the light of your own soul.
Look deep inside.
Be your own guide, and
Listen, listen, listen.

You have the answers
Only you know.
Trust your own truth, and
See your strength grow.
Just trust it, trust it, trust it.

Show the world who you are.
You have to sing your own song.
Don't wait too long.
Just sing it, sing it, sing it.

By Darlene Lancer

Contemplation

It's tempting to look outside ourselves for something or someone to take away our pain. We often flee from pain through distractions, relationships, addictions, or substances, seeking external solutions rather than addressing our inner struggles. Modern life, particularly in urban settings, disconnects us from our natural rhythms. The fast pace and demands of our culture, constant connectivity, and instant gratification overwhelm our biological makeup and detrimentally affect our emotional and physical health. This lifestyle can further distance us from true healing, exacerbating self-neglect and pain, so poignantly depicted in "Life's Playground."

Soul reclamation involves healing our broken hearts and wounds that interfere with our ability to love. An illusory search for a soul mate can bring sorrow, obscuring the truth that love resides within us. However, romantic disappointments open us to healing and transformation if we explore and grieve our longing.

Carl Jung believed that the longing for a romantic relationship is our soul's manifestation of a universal drive for wholeness. We can search endlessly for the one person who will make us feel complete and fulfilled, imagining that with the perfect mate, we will be healed and our yearning will end. This desire for a soul mate is an outer expression of an inner drive for a state of oneness, a return home, as described in "The One." We may glimpse this bliss in fleeting moments of unconditional love, sexual union, or divine connection. The angst of separation—whether from our beloved or internal peace—creates a sense of fragmentation, and longing inevitably returns.

Healing ourselves and our relationships begins and ends with self-love. Years ago I asked a teacher how to heal my pain. She simply replied, "You must learn to love yourself." I had no idea what she meant or how to achieve it. Over time I learned that self-love encompasses more than pampering ourselves; it involves a deep and compassionate understanding of who we are, communicating that, and setting appropriate boundaries both internally and with others.

Like change, healing takes courage, which requires a degree of confidence and determination. It demands that we slow down and take the time to heal ourselves from the inside out. This inward turn is the theme of "Turnaround." We must listen to, honor, and express our feelings. Ignoring or judging our body, needs, and feelings only prolongs our pain. Self-criticism sabotages self-esteem and worsens our misery. For example, while grief is a natural response to loss, guilt and self-blame create unnecessary suffering.

Two challenging aspects of self-love are self-care and self-nurturing. Many of us grow up with unmet emotional needs, making it difficult to recognize and respond to them later in life. If we lacked parental empathy as children, we may struggle to nurture ourselves as adults. We might be unaware of or dismiss our needs or not know how to meet them. The lack of an internal, loving parental voice to comfort ourselves can lead to anxiety, loneliness, addiction, and depression. We usually need support from someone who models self-nurturing skills to acquire them.

Self-care means not abandoning ourselves as we may have been abandoned by others. It involves meeting our emotional, social, and spiritual needs and protecting our physical and mental well-being. We need healthy nutrition, recreation, exercise, and adequate sleep. We must also be mindful of our thoughts and people that cause us stress and pain and learn to assertively set boundaries to safeguard our health.

Self-love also entails self-acceptance, meaning we allow who we are in the present moment. This doesn't preclude self-improvement, but it encourages compassion for ourselves, much like a nurturing parent would have shown us. Self-compassion expressed with gentleness, tenderness, and generosity of spirit is quite the opposite of self-criticism, perfectionism, and pushing ourselves.

Open your heart to whatever you're thinking and feeling. Notice your physical sensations. Give them space. This radical acceptance is an act of deep self-love. If you go deeper and merge with sensation, you discover it's merely flowing energy. The gentle embrace of your feelings creates a container that calms and reassures your being. It's an act of self-acceptance, demonstrated in "I'll Be There," which builds strength and inner peace to meet anything. Developing this habit may require frequent reminders, as expressed in "Soul Waters."

This approach is far different from self-pity, which judges our situation or feelings, suggesting, "It shouldn't be this way." If we judge and shame ourselves, we're at war with ourselves, and nothing changes. However, when we accept ourselves, we stop worrying about others' opinions and become more authentic. Acceptance allows us to reveal ourselves without shame or fear. As suggested in "Dear Heart," authenticity strengthens our true self.

Beyond attention, knowledge, acceptance, and self-compassion, self-love requires respect, responsibility, and commitment. It demands self-discipline, practice, and time. This may involve a significant reorientation of our values and our lives to focus less on external validation and more on inner contentment.

Faith and self-confidence help us comfort ourselves and navigate challenges and failures without lapsing into worry and self-judgment. We begin to know that we'll survive despite our present emotions. We won't develop this inner strength if we frequently pursue distractions and seek validation from others. Our ability to listen and trust the wisdom of our heart's whispers grows stronger with practice, as recounted in "My Ship Comes Home."

We often underestimate the impact of attentive listening and a loving response—to ourselves, our pain, and to others, even strangers. Extending love not only changes those around us but also furthers our growth. We have opportunities to practice self-love all the time, though it isn't easy. Our inner toddler or teenager rebels against self-responsibility. We may carry outdated, negative beliefs that thwart us.

Throughout the day, we have choices: To honor our feelings or dismiss them, to comfort or judge ourselves, to meet our needs or ignore them, to keep commitments to ourselves or abandon them, and to respect our values or override them. We abandon ourselves whenever we talk ourselves down, doubt ourselves, exhaust ourselves, dismiss our feelings or needs, or act against our values.

Conversely, making healthier choices fosters healing, benefiting both ourselves and our relationships. A loving gesture shifts our perception and brightens our days. When we approach life with heartfelt acceptance and compassion, it greets us in kind.

As you become empowered to "Follow Your Dreams," the world responds, doors open, and you experience the joy and aliveness of your authentic self.

About the Authors

Darlene Lancer is an international relationship expert and media spokesperson on narcissism, self-esteem, and codependency. She's a licensed psychotherapist, has counseled individuals and couples for over 35 years, and coaches internationally. Her books available in print, audio, and ebook, include:

Dating, Loving, and Leaving a Narcissist: Essential Tools for Improving or Leaving Narcissistic and Abusive Relationships

Codependency for Dummies

Conquering Shame and Codependency: 8 Steps to Freeing the True You.

Seven additional ebooks include: *10 Steps to Self-Esteem: The Ultimate Guide to Stop Self-Criticism, How To Speak Your Mind - Become Assertive and Set Limits, Spiritual Transformation in the Twelve Steps, "I'm Not Perfect - I'm Only Human" - How to Beat Perfectionism,* and *Freedom from Guilt and Blame - Finding Self-Forgiveness.*

In addition to her books, her insightful articles have been published in professional journals and numerous periodicals.

She had a successful career as an entertainment lawyer and was awarded a Juris Doctor and Phi Beta Kappa while at University of California at Los Angeles. She holds a Master's in Psychology from Antioch University.

Her books are available on Amazon, Smashwords, other booksellers, and her website, www.whatiscodependency.com, where visitors can also find audio and video resources and receive a free copy of "14 Tips for Letting Go." Follow her on Soundcloud, Clyp, LinkedIn, Youtube, X, Instagram, Bluesky, and Facebook.

To learn about events, seminars, and special offers, join her Mailing List.

Contributing Authors
(Listed Alphabetically)

Jason W. Brown is a neurologist and author of 16 books and hundreds of articles on neuropsychology and the philosophy of mind. You can learn more about him and his works at http://www.drjbrown.org. He currently lives with his wife in Fontareche, France.

Mike Gormley is a lyricist, journalist, and music artist's manager living in Los Angeles, known for bringing the Bangles, Danny Elman, and Oingo Boingo to international success. He hosts The Mike Gormley Show, a podcast about the music industry. Learn more about him at www.lapdev.com.

Ann Fuller is an artist in Oregon on a lifelong journey to trust the inner Light. Her art uses poetry, prose, images, and found objects to spread the word: "Nothing is wasted. Everyone has value."

Suzanne Henderson is a medical secretary, poet, and writer who lives in Cumbria, England. She has published her first poetry book *Life's Path* this year. You can see more of her writing at Medium.com/@suzannehenderson_6461.

David Morris is a retired Military and State Department veteran, suicide survivor, speaker, author, and mental health advocate. Originally from the Detroit metro area, he currently resides in Copenhagen, Denmark with his wife and 3 children.

Owen Reynolds is an engineer living in Irish midlands with his family, border collies, rabbits, and hens. He's an avid vintage car enthusiast and archer.

Ole Kevin Rodberg has studied film, English and social education, and works night shifts at a nursing home, while writing in his spare time. He lives in Oslo, Norway with his wife and two sons.

Porter Smith aka P.S. Lutz has an imagination that flows widely and evenly in musical and literary directions. He dedicates his artistic life to bridging distances between people and places far and wide. His website is https://pslutz.com.

Arianna Winkle is an artist living in Costa Rica with her dog Zoey. She enjoys photography, music, writing poetry, and practicing yoga. Her website is www.AriannaNoelle.com.

www.ingramcontent.com/pod-product-compliance
Lightning Source LLC
Chambersburg PA
CBHW071321130726
47996CB00002B/578